# Highlights™

## Laugh Attack!

# Wack-a-doodle School

## 1,001 Grade-A Riddles, Jokes, and Tongue Twisters

Illustrated by Pete Whitehead

Highlights Press
Honesdale, Pennsylvania

Copyright © 2015 by Highlights for Children, Inc.
All rights reserved.
For information about permission to reproduce selections from this book, please contact permissions@highlights.com.

Published by Highlights for Children, Inc.
P.O. Box 18201
Columbus, Ohio 43218-0201
Printed in the United States of America

ISBN: 978-1-62979-427-3

First edition

Visit our website at highlightspress.com.
10 9 8 7 6 5 4 3 2 1

Design by Dolores Motichka
Production by Sue Cole
The titles are set in Aachen Std Bold.
The text is set in Bones Regular.

# CONTENTS

School Sillies                        1

Language Laughs                      25

Math Mirth                           51

Music Cues and Art Smarts            79

School Tools                         99

Cafeteria Chuckles                  111

Rollicking Recess                   131

History Howlers                     145

Science Shenanigans                 171

Spoofy Sports                       195

Geography Gigglers                  215

Teacher Tee-Hee-Hees                237

# School Sillies

How do bees get to school?
*They take the school buzz.*

What do vampires wear on the first day of school?

*Their bat-to-school clothes.*

**TED:** I didn't know our school was haunted.

**NED:** Neither did I. How did you find out?

**TED:** Everybody's been talking about our school spirit!

Why did the dollar do so well in school?
*He was paying attention.*

How is school like taking a shower?
*One wrong turn and you're in hot water.*

**KENDRA:** Omar, were you late for school again?

**OMAR:** Yes, but didn't Mr. Macey say that it's never too late to learn?

What is a robot's favorite part of school?
*Assembly.*

**CHASE:** Were the test questions hard?

**CHERIE:** The questions were easy. It was the answers that gave me trouble!

What grades did the pirate get in school?
　　*High C's.*


Knock, knock.
*Who's there?*
Wafer.
*Wafer who?*
Wafer the bus at the corner.


Why didn't the zombie go to school?
　　*He felt rotten.*


Knock, knock.
*Who's there?*
Cheese.
*Cheese who?*
Cheese a very smart girl.

What do elves do after school?
   *Gnomework.*

Why did the student eat his homework?
   *Because the teacher told him it was a piece of cake.*

What did the father buffalo say to his kid when he dropped him off at school?

*"Bison."*

Why did the kid study in the airplane?

*He wanted a higher education.*

**TEACHER:** Where is your homework?

**AMAYA:** A ghost ate it.

**TEACHER:** I can see right through that excuse!

What did the bubble gum say when it failed its test?

*"I blew it."*

Why did the chicken stay home from school?

*It had the people pox.*

**TARA:** Why weren't you in school today?

**DARYL:** I had a toothache, so I went to the dentist.

**TARA:** Does your tooth still ache?

**DARYL:** I don't know. The dentist kept it.

**MOM:** Why didn't you take the bus home?

**ANDY:** I tried, but it wouldn't fit in my backpack.

Where does smart butter go?
*Honor roll (on a roll).*

How can you tell a school bus from a grape?
*Jump on one for a while. If you don't get any juice, it's a school bus.*

**MARK:** Do you like homework?

**MARIETTA:** I like nothing better.

What do librarians use as bait when they go fishing?
*Bookworms.*

Why did the cyclops stop teaching?
*Because he had only one pupil.*

Why didn't the sun go to college?
*Because it already had thousands
of degrees.*

Knock, knock.
*Who's there?*
Ketchup.
*Ketchup who?*
Ketchup or else you'll miss the school bus!

**TEACHER:** Why didn't you finish your homework?
**MONSTER:** I was full.

Why do fish know a lot?
*They swim in schools.*

What do you call a pirate who skips school?
*Captain Hooky.*

**BOOKS NEVER WRITTEN**

*Tardy* by Mark M. Late

*Long Walk Home* by Miss D. Bus

*Where to Sit in Class* by Wayne Front

*How to Not Succeed in School* by Skip Class

*When Does School Start?* by Wendy Belrings

*How to Stop Procrastinating* by Mae B. Later

*Summer School* by Nova Kayshon

*Smart People* by Gene E. Us

What's the hardest thing about falling out of bed on the first day of school?

*The floor.*

Why did the clock go to the principal's office?

*He was tocking too much.*

**DAD:** What did you learn in school today?

**DYLAN:** Not enough. I have to go back tomorrow!


Knock, knock.

*Who's there?*

Needle.

*Needle who?*

Needle little help with your homework?


**KARA:** My mom says that I get to choose my school clothes this year.

**SARA:** Oh, really? My dog's the one that chews mine!


What animal flies around schools at night?
*The alpha-bat.*

What is a bus you can never enter?
*A syllabus.*

What will the school for racecars do after the summer?
*Re-zoom.*

Why is the sun so bright?
*Because it shines in class.*

**EVANGELINE:** I got 100 in school today.
**DAD:** That's great! In what subject?
**EVANGELINE:** I got 50 in spelling and 50 in math.

Why did the dad have to go to school?
*To take his pop quiz.*

Why did the light bulb go to school?
*He wanted to get brighter.*


What animal peeks at other students' exams?
*The cheetah.*


**SCHOOL NURSE:** Have your eyes ever been
checked?

**CELIE:** No, they've always been blue.

What did the boy snail say to the girl snail at
the school dance?

*"I'm really good at slow dancing."*


How do sheep carry their homework?

*In baaackpacks.*

**JENNIFER:** Why were you late for school today?

**JEREMY:** I was dreaming about a football game, and it went into overtime.

Knock, knock.

*Who's there?*

Atlas.

*Atlas who?*

Atlas, it's the weekend!

Why was the phone put in an advanced class?

*Because it was a smartphone.*

**CARSON:** I just caught a school of fish.

**BILAL:** Great! What did you use to catch it?

**CARSON:** A bookworm.

Knock, knock.

*Who's there?*

Stacey.

*Stacey who?*

Stacey'ted until the bus stops.

Why did the boy bring his dad's credit card to school?

*He wanted extra credit.*

Why should you never dot another student's i's?

*You should always keep your i's on your own paper.*

Why didn't the nose want to go to school?

*Because he didn't want to get picked on.*

Why didn't the zombie go to school?

*Because he felt rotten.*

Why couldn't the invisible man pass summer school?

*Because the teacher always marked him absent.*


Where do flowers go to school?

*To the kinder-garden.*

Knock, knock.
*Who's there?*
Jewel.
*Jewel who?*
Jewel be sorry when the principal finds out.

Why was the dog so good in school?
*Because he was the teacher's pet.*

Where do fish learn to swim?
*In school.*


Why did the boy bring a ladder to school?
*He wanted to go to high school.*


How does a snowman get to school?
*By icicle.*


**PRINCIPAL:** Joanna, I hear that you missed the first day of school.

**JOANNA:** Yes, but I didn't miss it very much.


Why couldn't the flower go to school on its bike?
*Its petals (pedals) were broken.*

Why did the new boy steal a chair from the classroom?
*Because the teacher told him to take a seat.*

What do you call a duck that gets all A's in school?
*A wise quacker.*

## TONGUE TWISTERS

Ernest learned in earnest.

Bria brought a bright blue beret.

The class clock clicked clearly.

The quick, silver squid squealed at the
  quick quiz.

Vivien's vivid vests vex Vixen.

Misty missed marking Marvin's makeup quiz.

Brock's books break Blake's backpack.

# Language Laughs

What is an English teacher's favorite breakfast?
*A synonym roll.*

What do baby bunnies learn in school?
    *The alfalfa-bet.*

A teacher asked Old MacDonald, "How do you spell cow?"
He replied, "C-O-W-E-I-E-I-O."

**TEACHER:** Andrew, name two pronouns.

**ANDREW:** Who, me?

**TEACHER:** That's correct.


What color are books you've finished?
  *Read (red).*


**DARIA:** How do you spell elephant?

**DAN:** E-L-L-E-E-F-A-N-T.

**DARIA:** That's not how the dictionary spells it.

**DAN:** You didn't ask me how the dictionary spells it.


What comes after *L*?
  *Bow.*

What begins with *T*, ends with *T*, and
is full of *T*?
    *A teapot.*

**JESSICA:** What letter does *yellow* start with?
**NIKOLA:** *Y.*
**JESSICA:** Because I want to know!

A teacher was giving her class a grammar
lesson. "I ain't got a pet," she said. "How should
I correct that?"
    Julie raised her hand and said, "Buy a dog?"

What kind of bees do well in school?
    *Spelling bees.*

**DAD:** What did you learn in school today?

**MANNY:** My teacher taught us writing.

**DAD:** What did you write?

**MANNY:** I don't know. She hasn't taught us reading yet.

How is an English teacher like a judge?
*They both give out sentences.*

Why does it take pirates so long to learn the alphabet?

*Because they spend years at C.*

**BRYANT:** Where does Friday come before Thursday?

**DAD:** I don't know. Where?

**BRYANT:** In the dictionary!

Knock, knock.
*Who's there?*
Spell.
*Spell who?*
W-H-O.


What school did the alphabet go to?
   *LMNtary.*


**TEACHER:** Sam, come and write "mouse" on
   the board.
**SAM:** M-O-U-S.
**TEACHER:** What's on the end?
**SAM:** A tail!


Is there a word in the English language that
uses all the vowels including *Y*?
   *Unquestionably.*

**TEACHER:** Maddie, what letters do Tuesday, Thursday, Friday, and Saturday have in common?

**MADDIE:** They have no letters in common.

**TEACHER:** What? Yes they do.

**MADDIE:** No, none of them have *C, O, M,* or *N* in them!

What word becomes shorter when you add two letters to it?
  *Short.*

How do you make "one" disappear?
  *Add a G, and it's gone.*

**TEACHER:** Cory, your essay titled "My Dog" is similar to your brother's. Did you copy his?

**CORY:** No, miss, it is the same dog.

A woman sent her dog to college. The dog failed math but got an A in foreign languages. The woman said, "If you're so good at foreign languages, let me hear you say something in another language." The dog said, "Meow."

What word is always pronounced wrong?
*"Wrong."*

**TEACHER:** Give me a sentence using the words *defeat*, *defense*, and *detail*.

**NADIA:** Defeat of de dog went over defense before detail.

What do you say when comforting a grammar teacher?

"*There, their, they're.*"

**TEACHER:** Who can tell me what *N-E-V-E-R* spells?

**LIAM:** I can.

**TEACHER:** OK. Tell me.

**LIAM:** Never.

**TEACHER:** Please tell me now, or I will call your parents.

**LIAM:** Never!

How is a raven like a writing desk?
   *Edgar Allan Poe wrote on both of them.*


What kind of tree has poems on it?
   *A poetry.*

If you leave alphabet soup on the stove and
   go out, it could spell disaster.

**TEACHER:** Sarah, spell *vacuum*.

**SARAH:** *V-A-C-W-M.*

**TEACHER:** That's incorrect. There is no *W* in vacuum.

**SARAH:** I didn't say *W*. I said double *U*.



Knock, knock.

*Who's there?*

Thaddeus.

*Thaddeus who?*

To be or not to be. Thaddeus the question.



**ROMEO:** Juliet, dearest, I am burning with love for you.

**JULIET:** Come now, Romeo, don't make a fuel of yourself.

**BOOKS NEVER WRITTEN:**

*Pen Pals* by Anita Letterback

*How to Read Novels* by Paige Turner

*Detectives* by Mr. E.

*Learning the Alphabet* by Lotta Letters

*An Encyclopedia of Monsters* by Frank N. Stein

*How to Get Smart* by Reed A. Lot

Which hand is better to write with?
*Neither—you should use a pen!*

What kind of writing does a witch use?
*Cursive.*

What is heavy forward but not backward?

*Ton.*

**DIYA:** Can you spell *eighty* in two letters?

**MATTHEW:** Sure! *A-T.*

How do you spell *mousetrap*?

*C-A-T.*

**TEACHER:** How many letters are in the alphabet?

**AMANDO:** 11.

**TEACHER:** No, there are 26. How did you get 11?

**AMANDO:** *T-H-E A-L-P-H-A-B-E-T.*

What is a pronoun?

*A noun that gets paid.*

**TEACHER:** Give me a sentence starting with *I.*

**CORA:** OK. I is . . .

**TEACHER:** No, no. You do not say "I is." You say "I am."

**CORA:** OK. I am the ninth letter of the alphabet.

What is a witch's favorite subject in school? *Spelling.*

What is the world's longest punctuation mark? *The hundred-yard dash.*

**TEACHER:** Steven, give me a sentence that is a question.

**STEVEN:** Why do I always get the hard ones?

**TEACHER:** Very good.

How do spiders learn definitions?
*They use Web-ster's dictionary.*

Whoever said that words will never hurt
you has never been hit in the head with
a dictionary.

**JACKIE:** My teacher says that I have to write more clearly.

**MOM:** That's a good idea.

**JACKIE:** No, it isn't. Then she'll know I can't spell.

What speaks every language?
*An echo.*

What website did the English student go to for help with his homework?
*Grammar.comma.*

**NATALIE:** Hey, look! What is everyone doing at that punctuation party?

**JUSTIN:** I don't know, but they're hyphen fun!

What letter of the alphabet has lots of water?
*The C.*

What do elves learn in school?
*The elf-abet.*

What is smarter than a talking bird?
   *A spelling bee.*

Knock, knock.
*Who's there?*
Rita.
*Rita who?*
Rita book. It's fun!

**TEACHER:** Can you use the word *fascinate* in a sentence?

**ASHLEY:** Sure. I have ten buttons on my sweater, but I only fasten eight.

If the alphabet goes from *A* to *Z*, what goes from *Z* to *A*?
  *Zebra.*

What do you get when you put the letters *M* and *T* together?
  *Nothing—it's empty!*

**SCHOOL NURSE:** Have you ever had trouble with appendicitis?

**KWAME:** Only when I tried to spell it.

What starts with a *P*, ends with an *E*, and has a million letters in it?

*The post office.*

**RYAN:** Washington's wife went to Washington to watch Washington's washwoman wash Washington's wash. How many *W*'s are there in all?

**DEVON:** Ummm . . . 11?

**RYAN:** No, there are no *W*'s in *all*.

What is a ten-letter word that starts with gas?
*Automobile.*


**TEACHER:** Justice, can you use the words *pink carnation* in a sentence?

**JUSTICE:** If all the cars in America were pink, it would be a pink-car nation!


Knock, knock.
*Who's there?*
To.
*To who?*
No! It's "to whom."


What does the letter *A* have in common with a flower?

> *They both have bees (B's) coming after them.*

**ANJALI:** Can you spell a pretty girl with two letters?

**TRISTAN:** Q-T.

A boy said to his teacher one day, "Wright has not written 'write' right."

The teacher replied, "Right! Wright, write 'write' right, right away!"

What is the longest word in the English language?

*Smiles. There is a mile between the first letter and the last letter.*

When is a mailbox like the alphabet?

*When it's full of letters.*

## TONGUE TWISTERS

Brooke makes bookmarks.

Wally wrote rhymes.

Lowercase letters look less large than
uppercase letters.

Mark marks Brooke's books with bookmarks.

Commas cause pauses after clauses.

Lovely llamas love learning letters.

# Math Mirth

What was *T. rex*'s favorite number?
*Eight (ate).*

What do math teachers do in the lunchroom?
*They divide their lunches with one another.*


Why was the math teacher crying on the last day of school?
*Because he didn't want to be divided from his students.*

Knock, knock.

*Who's there?*

Tennis.

*Tennis who?*

Tennis five plus five.

**MICAH:** School is so confusing!

**DAD:** Why?

**MICAH:** Ms. Peterson said, "1 plus 9 equals 10, 6 plus 4 equals 10, and 7 plus 3 equals 10."

**DAD:** So?

**MICAH:** She won't make up her mind!

What did the math classroom have instead of desks?

*Times tables.*

How is 2 + 2 = 5 like your left foot?

*It's not right.*

**TEACHER:** Why did you write on your test that 10 times 2 is the same as 11 times 2?

**ADDISON:** Because 10 times 2 is 20, and 11 times 2 is 20, too (22).

What is a math teacher's favorite kind of candy?

*Measure-mints.*

**TEACHER:** Use the word *geometry* in a sentence.

**KADEN:** The little acorn grew and grew, and one day it awoke and said, "Gee-ahm-a-tree."

What did the plus sign say to the minus sign?
*"You are so negative."*

What do you call a soccer player who
loves arithmetic?
*A mathlete.*

**TEACHER:** If you had 27 marbles in one pocket and 89 in the other, what would you have?

**STACEY:** Heavy pants.

What is a butterfly's favorite subject at school? *Mothematics.*

How do you divide 16 apples evenly among 17 people?

*Make applesauce.*


If two is company and three is a crowd, what are four and five?

*Nine.*


Why did the girl wear glasses during math class?

*Because they improve di-vision.*


**AMAL:** Brr, I'm cold.

**BRIANA:** Just stand in a corner.

**AMAL:** How will that warm me up?

**BRIANA:** A corner is always 90 degrees.

Knock, knock.
*Who's there?*
Polly.
*Polly who?*
Polynomial.

What do you get when you divide the circumference of a jack-o'-lantern by its diameter?

*Pumpkin pi.*

**TEACHER:** What are 12 and 14?
**AIMEE:** Numbers.

What kind of meals do math teachers eat?

*Square meals.*

What did the 0 say to the 8?
*"Hey, nice belt!"*

What do you call a crushed angle?
*A rectangle (wrecked angle).*

**KIMIKO:** There are 60 fish in a fish tank, and 20 go on vacation. How many are left?

**LEXY:** Well, 60 minus 20 is—

**KIMIKO:** Stop counting. Fish don't go on vacation!

What subject do owls like to study?
*Owlgebra.*

How can you make seven even?
*Take away the S.*


**TEACHER:** Now class, I will ask you a question, and I want you all to answer at once. What is 7 plus 8?

**CLASS:** At once!


What snakes are good at doing sums?
*Adders.*


Why did the math student divide sin by tan?
*Just cos.*


Why did the two 4's skip lunch?
*They already 8 (ate).*

**BOB:** What's 5Q plus 5Q?

**TODD:** Ten Q.

**BOB:** You're welcome!

There are three kinds of mathematicians: those who can count and those who can't.

What do you call a number that can't keep still?
*A roamin' numeral.*

Why didn't the square talk to the circle?
*Because there wasn't a point.*

What tools do you need to do math?
*Multipliers.*

## BOOKS NEVER WRITTEN

*Math* by Adam Up

*Two Kinds of Numbers* by Evan N. Odd

*Shapes* by Paul E. Gone

*6 + 5 and Other Math Problems* by E. Leven

*Math Test* by Saul V. Problems

*The Numbers Game* by Cal Q. Later

What triangles are the coldest?
*Ice-osceles triangles.*


What is a math teacher's favorite sum?
*Summer.*

How many feet are in a yard?
*That depends on how many people are standing in it.*


How can you use 9 four times and make 100?
*99 9/9.*


What do you call an angle that is adorable?
*Acute angle.*


**TEACHER:** Jenna, if I gave you two goldfish and Markus gave you four goldfish, how many would you have?

**JENNA:** Eleven.

**TEACHER:** No, you would have six.

**JENNA:** But I already have five goldfish at home!

**AIDEN:** What is 2 plus 2?

**MOM:** 4?

**AIDEN:** For my math test!

What geometric figure is like a lost parrot?
*A polygon.*

What kind of tree does a math teacher climb?
*Geometry.*

**GRANDPA:** How many feet are in a mile?

**MOLLY:** That depends on how many people are running that mile.

What is a mathematician's favorite dessert?
*Pi.*

Why didn't the
quarter roll down
the hill with the nickel?
*Because it had
more cents.*

What did the 9 say to the 6?
*"Why are you standing on your head?"*

What do you call more than one *L*?
*A parallel.*

Why was 6 afraid of 7?
  *Because 7 8 9.*

**TEACHER:** If you got $20 from five people, what do you get?

**GEROME:** A new bike.

What is a forum?

*Two-um plus two-um.*

Why did the student do multiplication problems on the floor?

*The teacher told her not to use tables.*

**TEACHER:** If you had one dollar and then asked your dad for another dollar, how much money would you have?

**ELIZA:** One dollar.

**TEACHER:** Sorry, Eliza. It seems as if you don't know your addition.

**ELIZA:** I know addition, but you don't know my dad!

Why did the obtuse angle go to the beach?

*Because it was over 90 degrees.*

Knock, knock.
*Who's there?*
Vaughn.
*Vaughn who?*
Vaughn plus Vaughn equals two.

**TEACHER:** You have ten chocolate bars. You eat eight of them. What do you have now?
**ZANE:** A stomachache.

Why is arithmetic hard work?
*You have to carry all those numerals.*

**ANTON:** If I had three feet, what would I have?
**ALEC:** Trouble finding shoes!

What do you call people who like tractors?
*Protractors.*


Why is it dangerous to do math in the jungle?
*Because when you add four and four,*
*you get ate.*

**TEACHER:** Tiana, what's 2N plus 2N?

**TIANA:** I don't know, it's 4N (foreign) to me!

Why was the math book sad?
*Because it had too many problems.*

**TEACHER:** Mei, if a man walked three miles in one hour, how many could he walk in four hours?

**MEI:** That depends on how tired he got in the first hour!

Knock, knock.
*Who's there?*
Dozen.
*Dozen who?*
Dozen anyone want to let me in?

**NICO:** My dog is great at math.

**TEACHER:** Why do you say that?

**NICO:** I ask him what 2 minus 2 is.

**TEACHER:** 2 minus 2 is nothing.

**NICO:** That's exactly what he answers—nothing!

What do you get when you cross an algebra class with the prom?

*The quadratic formal.*

Why is a circle always hot?

*Because it is 360 degrees.*

**SURGEON:** Nurse, I have so many patients! Who do I work on first?

**NURSE:** Simple. Use the order of operations.


What kinds of numbers live in tall grass?

*Arithmeticks.*


Who invented algebra?

*An X-pert.*


Why didn't the geometry teacher come to school?

*Because she sprained her angle.*


Why should the number 288 never be mentioned?

*It's two gross.*

What did one calculator say to the other?

*"You can count on me."*

A woman has seven daughters, and each daughter has a brother. How many children does the woman have altogether?

*She has eight children.*

**TEACHER:** If three feet equals a yard, what is ten yards?

**ZALIKI:** A lot of grass to mow!

What do you call a pot of boiling water at the top of Mount Everest?

*A high-pot-in-use.*

## TONGUE TWISTERS

Sherman surely subtracts slowly.

Layla laid logs lengthwise.

Didi goes gaga over digits.

Addison adds several sevens.

Teachers teach times tables timely.

Simple subtraction simply stumps Steven.

Ed aided Addy in adding to eighty.

# Music Cues and Art Smarts

Why were the musical notes upset?
*Because they were right next to the*
*trouble (treble) clef.*

What is a statue's favorite type of cake?
  *Marble cake.*

Why couldn't the music teacher open his door?
  *Because his keys were on the piano.*

**JILL:** Was that you singing when I came in?

**JACKIE:** Yes. I was killing time before my lesson.

**JILL:** Well, you were definitely using the right weapon.

How are a train and an orchestra alike?
*They both have conductors.*

**PATRICK:** Dad, Mrs. Rickard gave me an F for this drawing.

**DAD:** She did? That's a great drawing! Why would she give you an F?

**PATRICK:** Because I drew it in French class.

What did the painting say to the detective?
*"It wasn't me. I was framed!"*

**BAND STUDENT:** Our school played Beethoven last night.

**GYM STUDENT:** Who won?

Knock, knock.
*Who's there?*
Mozart.
*Mozart who?*
Mozart is found in museums.

**COMPOSER:** It took me ten years to write this lullaby.

**PUBLISHER:** Why did it take so long?

**COMPOSER:** It kept putting me to sleep.

What is a pirate's favorite subject?
*Arrrrt.*

What's the difference between a fish
and a piano?

*You can tune a piano, but you can't tuna fish.*


Why could the artist cross the bridge
whenever he wanted to?

*Because it was a drawbridge.*

What is a music student's favorite food?
*Jam.*

What do artists use when they are sleepy?
*Crayawns.*

What do musicians do when they lose their beat?
*They have a tempo-tantrum.*

Why did the music teacher need a ladder?
*To reach the high notes.*

How does a tree draw a person?
*It makes a stick figure.*

What is a bumblebee's least favorite musical note?
*Bee flat.*

What is a cow's favorite school subject?
*Moosic.*

**JAYA:** Nurse, nurse! I was playing the harmonica in music class, and I swallowed it.

**SCHOOL NURSE:** You're lucky you weren't playing the piano!

What do you call a musical insect?
*A humbug.*

What is an art teacher's favorite berry?

*Crayonberries.*

What kind of coat is always wet when you put it on?

*A coat of paint.*

Knock, knock.

*Who's there?*

Sonata.

*Sonata who?*

Don't worry, sonata big deal.

**MBALI:** What happens if you're trying to drum but you don't know how?

**IAN:** Beats me!

**BOOKS NEVER WRITTEN:**

*How to Sing* by Mel O. Dee

*The Wonders of Woodwinds* by Clair E. Net

*Sing Out Loud* by Mike Rophone

*Perfectly Tuned* by P. Anno

*The Colors of the Rainbow* by Roy G. Biv

*Do It Yourself* by Art N. Craft

*Shades of Purple* by Violet Plumm

*Places of Masterpieces* by E. Zell

What is a balloon's least favorite music?
  *Pop.*


Why couldn't orange stay in rhythm with the other colors?
  *Because red and yellow were mixing him up.*

What is green and sings?
   *Elvis Parsley.*


**BAYLOR:** Why do you keep your music player
   in the refrigerator?

**TYLER:** Because I like cool music!


Why did Renoir become an Impressionist?
   *He did it for the Monet.*


When is a tuba good for your teeth?
   *When it's a tuba toothpaste.*


Where did the whale play his violin?
   *In the orca-stra.*

What did the artist say to the wall?
*"One more crack like that and I'll
plaster you."*

**DEREK:** Why are you plucking your guitar strings
with a pencil?

**JOSHUA:** I'm trying to write a song.

Knock, knock.

*Who's there?*

Benjamin.

*Benjamin who?*

Benjamin with the band all night.

What kind of pet can't be found at a pet store?
   *A trumpet.*

What kind of band doesn't make music?
   *A rubber band.*

**LYDIA:** Did you see that Van Gogh at
   the museum?

**NOLAN:** Yes, it sure drove by quickly.

What vegetable is in every song?
   *A beet (beat).*

Which parts of the body are the most musical?
*The organs.*


What kind of teacher teaches how to play the flute?
*A private tooter.*


**HECTOR:** The music teacher said I should sing tenor.

**MOM:** Tenor?

**HECTOR:** Ten or eleven miles away.


What is a music note's favorite sport?
*Beat-boxing.*


What do you call a hawk that can draw and play the guitar?
*Talonted.*

**NINA:** Will you draw me a horse and buggy?

**ARTY:** OK.

**NINA:** You only drew the horse.

**ARTY:** I thought the horse would draw
   the buggy.

How do you get 27 kids to carve a statue?
   *Just have everybody chip in.*

Why did Mozart get rid of his chickens?
*They kept saying, "Bach, Bach, Bach."*

**JASMINE:** I'm making a hundred dollars a night playing the violin.

**JON:** That's twenty-five dollars a string! If I were you, I'd play the harp.

How does the heart play music?
*It follows the beat.*

Knock, knock.
*Who's there?*
Statue.
*Statue who?*
It's me. Statue?

What's green and smells like blue paint?
*Green paint.*

**PIANO TUNER:** I'm here to tune your piano.

**CAITLIN:** I didn't call for a piano tuner.

**PIANO TUNER:** I know. Your neighbors did.

What dessert would you feed to a string quartet?
    *Cell-O.*

**VIOLINIST**: When can I use the practice room?

**PIANIST:** I'll be out in a minuet.

What did the artist say after he spilled paint on the boy?
    *"Are you all white?"*

Why couldn't Mozart find his teacher?
    *Because he was Haydn.*

## TONGUE TWISTERS

Patty prints pretty ponies.

Mark makes marker marks.

Drew draws dreadfully dreary drawings.

Pass the purple paint pot, please.

Sally sang simple songs softly.

The fair flutist flung fruit.

Many monkeys made maracas.

What kind of music do they play on
a space shuttle?
   *Rocket roll.*


**LULU:** I once sang "The Star-Spangled Banner"
   for three hours nonstop.
**WYATT:** That's nothing. I can sing "Stars and
   Stripes Forever."


If lightning strikes an orchestra, who is most
likely to get hit?
   *The conductor.*

# School Tools

What do you get when you throw books into the ocean?

*A title wave.*

Knock, knock.

*Who's there?*

Scissor.

*Scissor who?*

Scissor and Cleopatra.


**DICTIONARY:** Boo-hoo!

**MATH BOOK:** Why are you crying? I'm the one
with all the problems!


Where are pencils made?
*Pencil-vania.*

Who is the king
of the classroom?
*The ruler.*

What sheds skin but isn't alive?

*An eraser.*

**DANIEL:** What kind of pencil fixes cars?

**ENZO:** I don't know. What kind?

**DANIEL:** A mechanical pencil.

What did the cowboy say to the marker?

*"Draw, partner!"*

What did the pencil say to the paper?

*"I dot my i's on you."*

What do you get when you cross a piece of paper with a pair of scissors?

*A paper cut.*

What kind of berry can you use to draw?

*A crayonberry.*

**PEN:** Don't worry. Everything is going to be all "write!"

**PENCIL:** What's your point?

**PEN:** You look a little dull.

**PENCIL:** "Write" on! That's why I'm wearing this suit. Doesn't it make me look sharp?

What do you call a boy with a dictionary in his pocket?

*A smartypants.*

What is black when it's clean and white when it's dirty?

*A chalkboard.*

Why did the book go to the doctor?
*Because it hurt its spine.*

A girl came into a shop to buy a permanent marker. A few months later, she came back to return it. "I'd like my money back," she said. "You told me this was a permanent marker, but it already ran out of ink."

**AMIR:** Have you heard the story about the unsharpened pencil?

**PATTY:** No. How does it go?

**AMIR:** Nevermind. It's pointless.

How do you get straight A's?
*Use a ruler.*

What did the paper say to the pen?
*"Write on!"*

What do you call a book that only has pages with even numbers?
*Odd.*

What did the glue say to the paper?
*"Let's stick together."*

**A BOOK NEVER WRITTEN:**

*How to Draw* by Mark Er

*What Pencils Are For* by Megan Marks

*I Made a Mistake* by Anita Eraser

*Backpack Uses* by Carrie Books

*Calculator Powers* by Addison Numbers

Why did the chicken cross the book?
*To get to the author side.*

**ANNABELLE:** What brand of pencils do you want?
**KATHY:** I want brand-new pencils!

What did the
pencil sharpener
say to the pencil?
*"Stop going in circles and get to the point!"*

What did Natasha do when she saw the class rabbit eating the dictionary?

*She took the words right out of his mouth.*

What kind of pen wears a wig?

*A bald-point pen.*

**DUDE:** What is your horse's name?

**COWBOY:** I call him Ink.

**DUDE:** Why? He isn't black.

**COWBOY:** No, but he keeps running out of the pen.

Knock, knock.

*Who's there?*

Pencil.

*Pencil who?*

Your pencil fall down if you don't wear a belt.

What did the glue stick say to the eraser?

*Nothing. Glue sticks can't talk!*


What coin can you write with?

*A penny.*


What has three feet but no toes?

*A yardstick.*


**TEACHER:** Where is your pencil, Harmon?

**HARMON:** I ain't got none.

**TEACHER:** How many times have I told you not to say that? Now listen, "I do not have a pencil. You do not have a pencil. They do not have a pencil." Do you understand?

**HARMON:** Not really. What happened to all the pencils?

Priscilla packs purple pencils.

The blue glue grew green goo.

Stan staples Peter's papers.

Perfect piles of purple pencil shavings.

My marker makes messes.

Charlie chooses chalk; Prim prefers pencils.

Collin collects stickers for Stacey.

Percy pointed his pencil purposefully.

# Cafeteria Chuckles

What did one tray say to the other?
*"Lunch is on me today."*

What did the cafeteria clock do after eating its lunch?

*It went back four seconds.*

Knock, knock.

*Who's there?*

Cash.

*Cash who?*

No, thanks. I prefer peanuts.

What is a potato's least favorite day?
*Fry-day.*

Where do comedians go to eat lunch?
*The laugh-eteria.*

How do you make a cream puff?
*Take it jogging.*

**CAFETERIA WORKER:** We all need to eat greens every day. They're healthy for us.

**JIN:** OK. Can I have mint-chocolate-chip ice cream?

What stops a food fight in a cafeteria?
*A peas treaty.*

**MADDIE:** On a traffic light, green means go, yellow means wait, and red means stop, right?

**ELLE:** Yes.

**MADDIE:** Well, on a banana, green means wait, yellow means go, and red means, "Where did you get that banana?!"

What is the most adorable vegetable in the teacher's salad?

*The cute-cumber.*

What is bacteria?

*The rear entrance to a cafeteria.*

What do you get if you eat pasta while you're sick?

*Macaroni and sneeze.*

**MARINA:** I don't like all the holes in this Swiss cheese.

**CAFETERIA WORKER:** That's OK. Just eat around them and leave them on your plate.

What did one soup bowl say to the other?

*"You're soup-er."*

Why is an ice cube so smart?

*It has 32 degrees.*

**HOLLY:** Do you want the right half of this cookie?

**HAILEY:** Sure—I certainly don't want the wrong half!

Knock, knock.

*Who's there?*

Broccoli.

*Broccoli who?*

Broccoli doesn't have a last name, silly.

What is a school librarian's favorite food to barbecue?

*Shush-kabob.*

What did the cake say when it was raining ice?

*"It's icing!"*

A tomato, some lettuce, and some water
were in a race. The water was running,
the lettuce was a head, and the tomato
was trying to ketchup.

**JIMMY:** How do you eat your soup?

**KIMMY:** With my right hand.

**JIMMY:** That's funny. I use a spoon!

Why didn't the banana go to school?
*Because it wasn't peeling well.*

What did the computer do at lunchtime?
*It had a byte.*

**ELLA:** Did you hear the story about the cookie?

**BELLA:** No.

**ELLA:** That's OK. It was a crummy story anyway.

What kind of candy is always late for class?
*Choco-late.*

*Delicious Food* by Chris P. Bacon

*How to Make Bread* by Ryan Wheat

*Green Trees* by Brock A. Lee

*The Encyclopedia of Red Fruits* by Tom Ater

*Lunchmeat* by B. Loney

*Peanut Butter Lunches* by Sammy Chez

When is the best time to eat a banana?
*After it's peeled.*


When is the other best time to eat a banana?
*When the moment is ripe.*


What did the cheese say when he got his
school picture taken?
*"People!"*


What does a cookie say when it's excited?
*"Chip, chip, hooray!"*


**MOM:** Why did you just swallow the money
I gave you?
**TRAVIS:** You said it was my lunch money!

Why did the kid stare at his carton of orange juice?

*Because it said, "concentrate."*

Knock, knock.
*Who's there?*
Ice-cream soda.
*Ice-cream soda who?*
Ice-cream soda whole world will know how silly I am!

Why did the pickle go to the nurse's office?
*He felt dill.*

What did the green grape
say to the purple grape?
   *"Breathe!"*

Why are school cafeteria workers so mean?
   *Because they batter fish, beat eggs, and
   whip cream.*

What do sea monster students eat for lunch?
*Fish and ships.*

Knock, knock.
*Who's there?*
Howdy.
*Howdy who?*
How delicious are those cookies?

What number do you use to eat in the cafeteria?
*U-ten-sils.*

**GINGER:** Would you like my apple?

**JACK:** I don't feel like an apple.

**GINGER:** That's good. You don't look like an apple either.

**ALEX:** I packed my own lunch today.

**KELLY:** What did you bring?

**ALEX:** Uh . . . chocolate soup.

**KELLY:** Chocolate soup?

**ALEX:** Well, this morning it was ice cream.

Why was the apple lonely?
*Because the banana split.*


Knock, knock.
*Who's there?*
Mammoth.
*Mammoth who?*
Mammoth is sthuck 'cause I'th been eatin'
   peanut buther.


Why was the cafeteria's kitchen having
math problems?
*Its counter was gone.*


How did the egg cross the frying pan?
*It scrambled.*

**ROSEY:** Which do you like better, salt or pepper?

**DIEGO:** Pepper.

**ROSEY:** What? How insalting!

What did the ham do when he wanted to talk to the salami?

*He called a meat-ing.*

What did the pepperoni say when it needed to take notes?

*"May I have a pizza paper and a pen?"*

Knock, knock.

*Who's there?*

Fajita.

*Fajita who?*

Fajita another thing, I'll be stuffed.

Why was the oatmeal sad?
*No raisin (reason).*

How do you make a bean chili?
*You send it to the North Pole.*

What do you call cheese that isn't yours?
*Nacho cheese.*

Knock, knock.
*Who's there?*
Pudding.
*Pudding who?*
Pudding on your shoes before your pants
    is a bad idea.

**JANE:** Would you like a peeled grape?
**SARI:** No, thank you. It doesn't a-peel to me.

How do you make a strawberry shake?
    *By taking it to a scary movie.*

What is a tortilla chip's favorite dance?
    *Salsa.*

## TONGUE TWISTERS

Dish up double dips of spuds.

Crisscrossed crispy piecrust.

I see icy ice cream.

Paul picked a particular pickle.

Celia slurped spiced cider.

Seven lemon lollipops.

Parker's pappy packed peanuts.

# Rollicking Recess

Knock, knock.
*Who's there?*
Wanda.
*Wanda who?*
Wanda go on the swings with me?

What is the trombone's favorite thing on
the playground?
_The slide._

**TEACHER:** Amy, please use the word _lettuce_
in a sentence.

**AMY:** Please lettuce go to recess early today!

What does a piece of fruit say when it goes down a slide?

"Ki-wheee!"

Knock, knock.

*Who's there?*

Wood.

*Wood who?*

Wood you laugh at my jokes?

**ZOE:** I can make you say "purple."

**KASSIBI:** No, you can't!

**ZOE:** OK, say the colors of the American flag.

**KASSIBI:** Red, white, and blue.

**ZOE:** That's right.

**KASSIBI:** But you said you'd make me say purple.

**ZOE** There, you just said it!

Knock, knock.

*Who's there?*

Nuisance.

*Nuisance who?*

What's nuisance yesterday?

**LARRY:** What does IDK mean?

**MITCH:** I don't know.

**LARRY:** You're the fifth person I've asked. Nobody knows what it means!

**MEIRA:** Have you heard the joke about the jump rope?

**ELI:** No.

**MEIRA:** Skip it.

Knock, knock.

*Who's there?*

Hatch.

*Hatch who?*

Ha ha, made you sneeze!


Why did the chicken cross the playground?

*To get to the other slide.*


There was once a boy in school whom the other kids thought they could trick. Every day one of the kids would put a dime in one hand and a quarter in the other, then ask the boy to pick the one he wanted. Every day the boy would pick the dime. One day a girl who was watching this asked the boy why he kept taking the dime.

"Well," the boy replied, "if I took the quarter, they'd stop doing it."

**ZACHARY:** Do you want to hear a long joke?

**KAYLA:** Sure.

**ZACHARY:** Jooooooooke.

What's the most expensive game of tag?
*Price tag.*

**CARA:** I can tell you what the score will be before the kickball game starts.

**CORY:** No way!

**CARA:** Yes, I can. 0–0. It hasn't started yet!

Knock, knock.
*Who's there?*
Toucan.
*Toucan who?*
Toucan play this game.

Knock, knock.
*Who's there?*
Canoe.
*Canoe who?*
Canoe come and
  play with me?

**KATHERENE:** Hey, Kati, can you answer a question
  for me?

**KATI:** Sure!

**KATHERENE:** Thanks.

**MARGIE:** What was that loud noise?

**ALICE:** My jacket fell on the floor.

**MARGIE:** Why did your jacket make such a
  loud noise?

**ALICE:** Because I was wearing it when it fell.

A man escaped from prison by digging a hole. After hours of digging, he saw he was in a playground. He leaped in the air and said, "I'm free! I'm free!" A little girl walked up to him and said, "So what? I'm four."

**SHILOH:** I know how to keep a person in great suspense.

**ROYA:** How?

**SHILOH:** Tell you tomorrow.

Knock, knock.
*Who's there?*
Spin.
*Spin who?*
Spin too long since we saw each other.

Why can't Dalmatians play hide-and-seek?
*They will always be spotted.*

Where do explorers go to play?
*A jungle gym.*

A kid was walking to the swings when suddenly he stopped and looked at the sky. Another saw him, stopped, and did the same thing. More students came by and also looked at the sky. Finally, the second kid asked the first kid, "What are you looking at?"

The first kid said, "I don't know about you, but I have a nosebleed!"

**PHIL:** Santa decided to give his reindeer a year off, so he got eight monkeys to pull his sleigh—Do, Re, Fa, So, La, Ti, and Do.

**WILL:** What about Mi?

**PHIL:** Oh, are you a monkey, too?

Knock, knock.

*Who's there?*

Freddie.

*Freddie who?*

Freddie or not, here I come.

**BRIANNA:** You won't believe what happened today.

**ANDREW:** What?

**BRIANNA:** The weather forecast said it was going to be chilly, so my brother ran outside with a bowl and said, "Where's the chili?"

Knock, knock.
*Who's there?*
Little old lady.
*Little old lady who?*
Wow—I didn't know you could yodel!


**JENNIFER:** Do you want to hear a bird joke?
**JADE:** No, thanks.
**JENNIFER:** Well, this is "hawk"ward . . .


Why didn't the skeleton like recess?
   *He had no body to play with.*


Knock, knock.
*Who's there?*
Meter.
*Meter who?*
Let's meter at the slide.

## TONGUE TWISTERS

Silly Sally always slides sideways.

Quick! Switch wristwatches.

Juggling jaguars jumped on the jungle gym.

Wesley sings as Leslie swings.

Hillie's hopscotch had Hannah
hopping happily.

Reese's recess rocked.

Sarah slid down several slides.

# History Howlers

Why is England the wettest country?
*Because the queen
has reigned there
for years.*

What is a snake's favorite subject?

*Hiss-tory.*

**TED:** What's the difference between a duck and George Washington?

**LEYLA:** I don't know. What?

**TED:** A duck has a bill on its face, and George Washington has his face on a bill.

Knock, knock.

*Who's there?*

Tarzan.

*Tarzan who?*

Tarzan stripes forever.

If April showers bring May flowers, what do May flowers bring?

*Pilgrims.*


What did King Arthur say to his court?

*"I want all of you to enroll in knight school."*


What did Paul Revere say when he went to the orthodontist?

*"The braces are coming! The braces are coming!"*


**MOM:** Why aren't you doing well in history class?

**CHRIS:** Because the teacher keeps asking about things that happened before I was born!

How did the Vikings send secret messages?
*By Norse code.*


Who invented fractions?
*Henry the 1/4th.*


**TEACHER:** What important even happened in 1809?

**MATT:** Abraham Lincoln was born.

**TEACHER:** Correct. Now what important event happened in 1812?

**MATT:** Abraham Lincoln had his third birthday.


Why was it easy to celebrate Mother's Day in ancient Egypt?
*Because there were so many mummies.*

Who was purple and conquered the world?
*Alexander the Grape.*

**TEACHER:** What did the American colonists do
at the Boston Tea Party?

**LILY:** I don't know. I wasn't invited!

What was the most popular dance in 1776?
*Indepen-dance.*

What do presidents eat to freshen their breath?
*Govern-mints.*

Why does the Statue of Liberty stand in New York Harbor?

*Because she can't sit down.*

What did Caesar say to Cleopatra?

*"Toga-ether we can rule the world!"*

**SHAUN:** I wish I had been born 1,000 years ago.

**CASSY:** Why is that?

**SHAUN:** Just think of all the history that I wouldn't have to learn!

Why were the early days of history called the dark ages?

*Because there were so many knights.*

What kind of music did the Pilgrims like?
*Plymouth Rock.*


A king has three cups. Two of the cups are filled with water. What is the king's name?
*King Fill-up the Third (Philip the 3rd).*


How did Columbus's men sleep on their ships?
*With their eyes shut.*


**BENJAMIN:** Did you know that Abraham Lincoln had to walk miles to school every day?

**THOMAS:** Well, he should have gotten up earlier and caught the school bus like everyone else!

Why are politicians always in such a hurry?
*Because they have to run for office.*

What do you get when you cross a U.S.
president with a shark?
*Jaws Washington.*

What does the president use to decorate the White House for the Fourth of July?

*The Decorations of Independence.*

Knock, knock.

*Who's there?*

General Lee.

*General Lee who?*

General Lee I do not tell knock-knock jokes.

**DAD:** How is your report card, Maria?

**MARIA:** Well, Dad, I did the same thing as George Washington.

**DAD:** And what is that?

**MARIA:** I went down in history.

**BOOKS NEVER WRITTEN**

*Who Was George Washington?* by
 Perez E. Dent

*A Leap for Mankind* by Landon Moon

*Life in the 1800s* by Noah Lectricity

*Signing the Declaration of Independence* by
 Phil A. Delphia

*Ancient Egyptian Marvels* by P. Ramid

*Thoughts of the Wright Brothers* by Ike N. Fly

*The First U.S. State* by Della Ware

What did Benjamin Franklin say when he flew
a kite in a lightning storm?
*Nothing—he was too shocked.*

**ADITYA:** If Mrs. Green lives in a green house, Ms. Blue lives in a blue house, and Mr. Red lives in a red house, who lives in the White House?

**CARLY:** Mr. White?

**ADITYA:** No, the president of the United States!

Who un-invented the airplane?
*The Wrong brothers.*

Which U.S. president liked the environment?
*Tree-adore (Theodore) Roosevelt.*

**LEAH:** Why did George Washington chop down the cherry tree?

**RACHAEL:** I'm stumped.

Who built King Arthur's round table?
*Sir Cumference.*

What do Alexander the Great and Kermit the Frog have in common?

*The same middle name.*

**CANDICE:** Why was the pharaoh boastful?

**LARRY:** I don't know. Why?

**CANDICE:** Because he sphinx he's the best.

One day, a man asked the president if he could have the country for free. The president said no. "Why not?" the man asked. "I thought it was a free country!"

How many ears did Davy Crockett have?

*Three—a left ear, a right ear, and a wild frontier.*

Which American president wore the
biggest hat?

*The one with the biggest head.*

Who was the biggest thief in history?

*Atlas. He held up the whole world!*

What was Camelot?

*A place where people parked their camels.*

How was the Roman Empire cut in half?
*With a pair of Caesars.*

**LARA:** Did you hear the one about the Liberty Bell?

**LANCE:** Yeah, it cracked me up!

What did the knight's tombstone say?

*"Rust in peace."*

Knock, knock.

*Who's there?*

Teachers.

*Teachers who?*

Teachers (three cheers) for the red, white, and blue.

Where was the Declaration of Independence signed?

*At the bottom.*

**ROMAN SOLDIER #1:** What time is it?

**ROMAN SOLDIER #2:** It's XX past VII.

**KATE:** Two wrongs don't make a right, but what do two rights make?

**MOM:** I don't know. What?

**KATE:** Two Wrights make an airplane!

Who succeeded the first president of the United States?

*The second one.*

What do you call an American drawing?

*A Yankee doodle.*

**TEACHER:** For homework tonight, I want you to write an essay on George Washington.

**BART:** I'd rather write on paper.

Where did Montezuma
go to college?
*Az Tech.*

Why did Columbus cross the ocean?
*To get to the other tide.*

Why did the pioneers cross the country in covered wagons?
*Because they didn't want to wait 40 years for a train.*

Where did people dance in medieval times?
*In knight clubs.*

Knock, knock.

*Who's there?*

Unite.

*Unite who?*

When unite Lancelot, he joins the Round Table.

What do history teachers make when they want to get together?

  *Dates.*

What kind of tea did the American colonists like?

  *Liberty.*

What famous inventor loved practical jokes?

  *Benjamin Pranklin.*

Who was the biggest jokester in George Washington's army?

*Laughayette.*

Why did Arthur have a round table?

*So no one could corner him!*

Knock, knock.

*Who's there?*

Llama.

*Llama who?*

"Llama Yankee Doodle Dandy."

What explorer was the best at hide-and-seek?

*Marco Polo.*

**MADELEINE:** What rank was the popcorn in the army?

**BHAVANI:** I don't know. What?

**MADELEINE:** A colonel (kernel). Did you like this joke?

**BHAVANI:** It was pretty corny.

**MADELEINE:** Really? I thought it popped!

Why did Julius Caesar buy crayons?
*He wanted to Mark Antony.*

How were the first Americans like ants?
*They lived in colonies.*

**TEACHER:** Do you know the sixteenth president of the United States?

**SANDRA:** No, we were never introduced!

What did Mason say to Dixon?
*"We've got to draw the line here."*

How do you find King Arthur in the dark?
*With a knight light.*

Washington wished for white whiskers.

Paul Revere rode to reveal the arriving British.

The president proposed posing proudly
  in the picture.

Nervous knights never knock noisily.

Pilgrims plucked plump, purple plums.

# Science Shenanigans

What is a volcano's favorite food?
*Magma-roni and cheese.*

**NIKITA:** Anyone know any jokes about sodium deposits?

**TAYLOR:** Na.

What is root beer's favorite subject?
  *Fizzics (physics).*

What did the white blood cell say to the other white blood cells?
  *"Antibody out there?"*

What does a rain cloud wear under its clothes?
  *Thunderwear.*

Where do geologists like to relax?
  *In a rocking chair.*

Knock, knock.

*Who's there?*

Element.

*Element who?*

Element to tell you that she can't see you today.

**SAM:** Did you hear the joke about the rocket?

**BEN:** No, what is it?

**SAM:** It's out of this world!

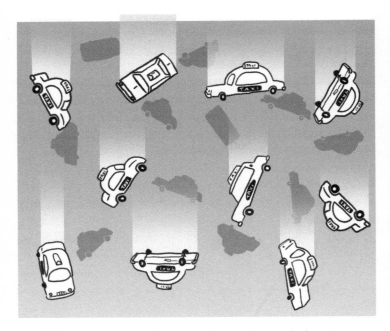

What is worse than raining cats and dogs?
*Hailing taxis.*


**CAMILA:** Guess what I've had stuck in my head
for a long time?

**ABBY:** What?

**CAMILA** My brain!

**WATSON:** Holmes! What kind of rock is this?

**HOLMES:** Sedimentary, my dear Watson.

How do eyes communicate with each other?
*They use contacts.*

**VAL:** Did you hear about the scientist who was reading a book about helium?

**VINCENT:** Yes. He just couldn't put it down.

Knock, knock.
*Who's there?*
Comet.
*Comet who?*
Comet a crime, go to jail.

What did the boy volcano say to the girl
volcano?

*"I lava you!"*

What fruit contains barium and double
sodium?

*BaNaNa.*

Why can't your nose be 12 inches long?

*Because then it would be a foot.*

**ASHLEY:** If a red house is made out of red
bricks and a blue house is made out of
blue bricks, what is a greenhouse made
out of?

**DAD:** Green bricks?

**ASHLEY:** No, a greenhouse is made out of glass!

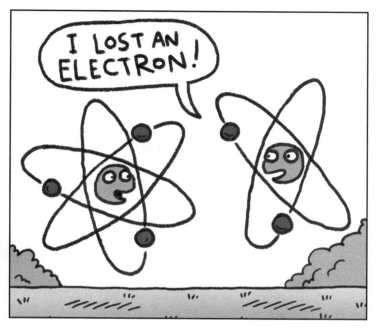

Two atoms were walking down the street. One said, "I lost an electron!"

"Are you sure?" asked the other.

"I'm positive," said the first.

How do you know the moon is going broke?

*It's down to its last quarter.*

Why was there thunder and lightning in the science lab?

*The scientists were brainstorming.*

What did the paper clip say to the magnet?
*"You're so attractive!"*

**MEGAN:** What's the matter?
**MADDIE:** Anything that has mass and weight.

The little tree got worried in October because all his leaves fell off. But when spring came, he was re-leaved.

Where do scientists read facts about volcanoes?
*In magma-zines.*

What's the difference between weather and climate?
*You can't weather a tree, but you can climate.*

**TEACHER:** Donald, what is the chemical formula for water?

**DONALD:** *H-I-J-K-L-M-N-O.*

**TEACHER:** That's incorrect.

**DONALD:** But yesterday you said it was *H* to *O*.

What kind of knot do you tie in space?
*An astro-knot (astronaut).*

What do marine biologists enjoy doing most at sports games?
*The wave.*

What do female chromosomes use to look pretty?
*Genetic makeup.*

**BOOKS NEVER WRITTEN**

*How to Save the Planet* by Reese Ikle

*The Water's Surface* by Al G.

*The Moon in the Sky* by Myles A. Way

*Floating Furniture* by Aunty Gravity

*The Place of Disasters* by Milo Boratory

*All about Atoms* by Molly Cule

*Strong Bones* by Cal C. Uhm

*The Bottom of the Ocean* by Vera Deepe

**SOPHIA:** Dad, which planet is closest to us?

**DAD:** I think it is Venus.

**SOPHIA:** No, silly, it's Earth!

What is a tornado's favorite game?
*Twister.*

What's wrong with a joke involving cobalt, radon, and yttrium?

*It's CoRnY.*

Why didn't the scientist put a bell on his door?

*He wanted to win the no-bell prize.*

Knock, knock.

*Who's there?*

Jupiter.

*Jupiter who?*

Jupiter fly in my soup?

What did one eye say to the other?

*"Between you and me, there's something that smells!"*

**SCIENTIST #1:** We have discovered that exercise will help kill germs.

**SCIENTIST #2:** But how in the world are we going to get germs to exercise?

What is the opposite of a hurricane?
*A him-icane.*

Why is lava red hot?
*Because if it were cold and white, it would be snow.*

**TEACHER:** Joe, please give me a sentence that uses the word *buoyant.*

**JOE:** The girl ant was in love with the boy ant.

What did the comet say to the sun?
  *"See you next time around!"*


What do you call a million-year-old dinosaur?
  *A fossil.*


What is the Earth after it rotates all day?
  *Dizzy.*

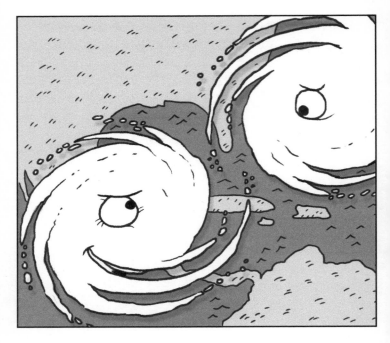

What did one hurricane say to the other?
*"I have my eye on you."*

**JAMAL:** Have you heard the joke about the flu?

**DANIELLE:** No, what is it?

**JAMAL:** Never mind. I don't want to spread it.

**TEACHER:** Harly, please give me the definition of climate.

**HARLY:** That's what a kid does when he sees a tree!

How does the man on the moon hold up his pants?
*With an asteroid belt.*

What did one volcano say to the other?
*"Stop int-erupt-ing me!"*

Why does lightning shock people?
*Because it doesn't know how to conduct itself.*

Why do mushrooms look like umbrellas?
*Because they grow in damp places.*

A neutron walked into a restaurant and ordered a soft drink.

"How much?" he asked.

"For you? No charge," the waiter said.


If a moth breathes oxygen in the daytime, what does it breathe at night?

*Nightrogen.*


**NNEOMA:** Which runs faster—hot or cold?

**NATALIE:** I don't know. Which?

**NNEOMA:** Hot! Anyone can catch a cold.


What did the molecule's mom say to him every morning?

*"Up and atom!"*

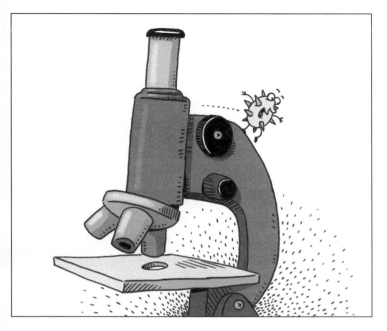

Why did the germ cross the microscope?
*To get to the other slide.*


What is an astronaut's favorite key on the
computer keyboard?
*The space bar.*

What metal makes the best boss?
  *Lead.*

What do you call sleeping twisters?
  *Tornadoze.*

How do you build a house in outer space?
  *You planet (plan it).*

What can go through water and not get wet?
  *Sunlight.*


Knock, knock.
*Who's there?*
Atomic.
*Atomic who?*
I have atomic ache.


Why is the nose in the middle of your face?
  *Because it's the scenter.*


**ASTRONAUT #1:** If you look down, I think you can
  see China.
**ASTRONAUT #2:** You've got to be kidding.
  The next thing I know, you'll tell me I can
  see knives and forks, too.

What is a volcano?

*A mountain with hiccups.*

What kind of gum do scientists chew?

*Ex-spearmint gum.*

Shiny, shimmering, silver stars.

Clem clamored for climate change.

In outer space spin great galaxies.

The twisting tornado turned toward two trees.

Kent keeps Cam's chemicals carefully contained.

The scientist's experiment exceeded expectations.

The tree roots reached right round the rock.

# Spoofy Sports

What is the loudest kind of sports equipment?
*A racket.*

**ALEXIS:** I wish I could bowl as well as I can bat.

**LEAH:** How well can you bat?

**ALEXIS:** All I ever get are strikes!

What do pigs do when they play basketball?
*They hog the ball.*

Why do soccer players do so well in school?
*They use their heads.*


Why did the football coach go to the bank?
*To get his quarterback.*


What is a banana's favorite gymnastic move?
*The banana split.*


**MRS. COLLINS:** Li, how do you like trampolining in P.E.?

**LI:** Oh, up and down, you know.


What did the bumble bee soccer player say after he kicked the ball into the net?
*"Hive scored!"*

What has eighteen legs and catches flies?
*A baseball team.*

**DAD:** Time to get up, Joe. It's five to eight.
**JOE:** Who's winning?

Why did the triangle jog around the block?
*To get into shape.*

What do you do if the basketball court gets flooded?

*Call in the subs.*

**GINA:** I'm a good swimmer. I've been swimming since I was five years old.

**RAMON:** You must be tired!

A team of little animals and a team of big animals decided to play football. During the first half of the game, the big animals were winning. But during the second half, a centipede joined the game, and the little animals started to catch up. The centipede scored so many touchdowns that the little animals won the game. When the game was over, the chipmunk asked the centipede, "Where were you during the first half?"

"Putting my shoes on," the centipede said.

Why did the ghost get kicked out of the football game?

*Because he screamed, "Boo!"*

Why don't golfers usually drink coffee?

*They always carry tees.*

**COACH:** Out of twenty teams in the league, our team finished last.

**BOWLER:** Well, it could have been worse.

**COACH:** How?

**BOWLER:** There could have been more teams in the league.

What did one golfer say to the other?

*"May the course be with you."*

Which athletes are the sloppiest eaters?
*Basketball players, because they're always dribbling.*

What did the glove say to the baseball?
*"Catch you later!"*

Why did the football coach send in his second string?

*To tie up the game.*

**BASEBALL PLAYER:** How do I exit the stadium?

**UMPIRE:** Three strikes and you're out.

What should you drink when you're watching your favorite sports game?

*Root beer.*

What did Count Dracula's baseball team call him when he hit a home run?

*A champire.*

How does a tennis shoe sneeze?

*"A tennis shoe! A tennis shoe!"*

**BOOKS NEVER WRITTEN**

*Running the Mile* by Otto Breath

*Where to Kick the Ball* by Indy Net

*Places to Exercise* by Jim Nasium

RUNNING THE MILE

BY OTTO BREATH

What kind of insects are bad at football?
*Fumblebees.*

**ERIN:** What is the quietest sport?
**ELENI:** Bowling, of course. You can hear a pin drop!

**DAD:** How did you do in the football game today?

**TIM:** I made a 92-yard run.

**DAD:** That's great!

**TIM:** Not really. I didn't catch the guy I was chasing.

What time of year is it best to use a trampoline?

*In the springtime.*

Which baseball player is in charge of the lemonade?

*The pitcher.*

What kind of plant is good at gymnastics?

*Tumbleweed.*

**NIKKI:** Dad, I can't find my baseball mitt.

**DAD:** Maybe it's in the car.

**NIKKI:** I looked there already.

**DAD:** Did you check the glove compartment?

What do you call a ball that wears a sock?
   *A football.*

What would you get if you crossed a bowling alley with a knitting class?
   *Pins and needles.*

**PHIL:** Where are you taking that skunk?

**BILL:** To the gym.

**PHIL:** What about the smell?

**BILL:** Oh, he'll get used to it.

Why is the football stadium so hot after the game?

*All the fans are gone!*

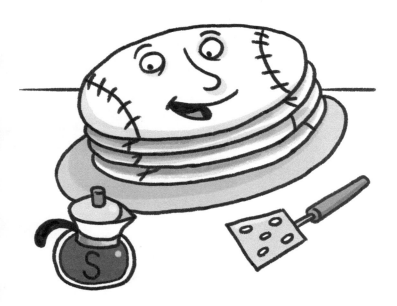

What do baseball and pancakes have in common?

*They both need the batter.*

What kind of bow can't be tied?
*A crossbow.*

Why is a tennis court so noisy?
*Because everyone raises a racket.*

**TEACHER:** Cameron, what are the four seasons?
**CAMERON:** Baseball, football, hockey, and vacation!

"That kid is my wonder player," said the coach, looking at a boy who kept missing the ball.

"How can that be?" asked the assistant coach. "He keeps messing up."

"Yeah," said the coach. "I often wonder whether he'll ever catch the ball."

Why is Cinderella bad at basketball?
*Because she runs away from the ball.*


What is a cake's position in baseball?
*Batter.*

What do you get if you cross a dinosaur and a football player?

*A quarterback no one can tackle.*

What do runners do when they forget something?

*They jog their memory.*

What position does a dog play on the football field?

*Rufferee.*


Why do tires get upset when they go bowling?

*Because they never make strikes, just spares.*


**DINAH:** Are you a good soccer player?

**VIOLET:** I'm so good I can play without using my hands.


What flavor of ice cream do bikers like the least?

*Rocky road.*


Why is a basketball game equal to a dollar?

*Both are made up of four quarters.*

**FRAN:** I sure liked the football game yesterday.

**DAN:** I did, too, but what was all the fuss about twenty-five cents?

**FRAN:** What do you mean?

**DAN:** Well, every time somebody caught the ball, the people yelled, "Get the quarterback! Get the quarterback!"

What kind of race is never run?

*A swimming race.*

In what sport do you sit down going up and stand up going down?

*Skiing.*

Where do joggers take baths?

*In running water.*

# Geography Gigglers

Where are the Great Plains?
*At the great airports.*

Whar is purple, long, and 50,000 years old?
*The Grape Wall of China.*

What is the smartest state?
*Alabama, because it has four A's and one B.*

What state do lions like best?
*Maine (mane).*


Knock, knock.
*Who's there?*
Juneau.
*Juneau who?*
Juneau where Alaska is?


**TEACHER:** Jeremy, please use the word *denial* in a sentence.

**JEREMY:** Denial is a river in Egypt.


What rock group has four men that don't sing?
*Mount Rushmore.*

Knock, knock.
*Who's there?*
Frances.
*Frances who?*
Frances in Europe.

**RENATA:** If Mississippi bought Virginia a New Jersey, what would Delaware?

**LIAM:** Idaho . . . Alaska!

What is the worst thing that can happen to a geography teacher?
*Getting lost.*

What is the capital of Washington?
*W.*

**BRITTANY:** What famous structure keeps falling?

**TEACHER:** The Leaning Tower of Pisa?

**BRITTANY:** No, the I-fell (Eiffel) Tower!

Knock, knock.

*Who's there?*

Albany.

*Albany, New York?*

No, Albanying help with my homework!

What mountain is the laziest?
*Mount Ever-rest.*


Why does the Yeti know all the map symbols?
*Because he's a legend.*


**TEACHER:** Liza, what is your favorite state?

**LIZA:** Mississippi.

**TEACHER:** Wonderful! Spell it, please.

**LIZA:** Oh, my favorite state? I meant to say Ohio.


Knock, knock.
*Who's there?*
Europe.
*Europe who?*
I can tell Europe to no good.

**BOOKS NEVER WRITTEN**

*Enjoying the Sunshine* by Cal E. Fornia

*The Mount Everest Challenge* by Clem Montin

*The Land of 10,000 Lakes* by Minnie Sota

*Are We There Yet?* by Mindy Carr

*The Coldest Continent* by Aunt Arctica

*Potato Legends* by Ida Ho

*Two Texas Cities* by Austin N. Dallas

*Touring Arizona* by Gran Canyon

*Exploring the Country* by Wanda Rhode

What is the fastest country in the world?
*Rush-a (Russia).*

Knock, knock.
*Who's there?*
Paris.
*Paris who?*
A Paris good, but I'd rather have an orange.

What state asks a lot of questions?
  *Why-oming.*


What group of mountains is a fruit?
  *The Apple-acian Mountains.*


**REILLY:** Have you guys seen Los Angeles?
**MALIK AND STEPH:** How could we? She's lost, isn't she?


What's big and white and lives in the Sahara Desert?
  *A lost polar bear.*


What state has the most streets?
  *Rhode (road) Island.*

What is the coldest country in South America?
*Chile.*


**TEACHER:** Aisha, can you tell me where the
North and South Poles are?

**AISHA:** I'd have to go the ends of the of the
Earth to answer that!


Which is smarter, longitude or latitude?
*Longitude, because it has 360 degrees.*


**TEACHER:** Marie, please go to the map and
point to Cuba.

**MARIE:** Here it is!

**TEACHER:** Very good. Now, does anyone know
who discovered Cuba?

**DEREK:** Marie!

**TEACHER:** Becky, where is Moscow?

**BECKY:** In the barn next to Pa's cow.

What kind of flower do geographers grow
in their gardens?

*Compass roses.*

**TEACHER:** Reid, where is the English Channel?

**REID:** I don't know. My TV doesn't pick it up!

What state is round at each end and high in the middle?

*Ohio.*

Knock, knock.
*Who's there?*
Kenya.
*Kenya who?*
Kenya guess who it is?

What do maps and fish have in common?

*Both have scales.*

Knock, knock.
*Who's there?*
Iowa.
*Iowa who?*
Iowa you a dollar.

**TEACHER:** Jaime, what can you tell me about the Dead Sea?

**JAIME:** I didn't even know it was sick!

Knock, knock.
*Who's there?*
Hawaii.
*Hawaii who?*
Hawaii doing today?

**HANNAH:** Did you hear about the four new states?

**OLIVIA:** What four new states?

**HANNAH:** New York, New Hampshire, New Mexico, and New Jersey.

What is the capital of Alaska?
*Come on, Juneau this one!*

What's big, white, furry, and always points north?
*A polar bearing.*


**TEACHER:** Reina, can you name two famous poles?
**REINA:** I can name three! North, South, and tad.

Knock, knock.

*Who's there?*

Florida.

*Florida who?*

The Florida bathroom is wet.

What's a pirate's favorite country?
*AAARRRgentina.*


What did Mississippi sip?
*A Minnesota (mini soda).*


It's suppertime and I'm Hungary. So I Russia downstairs, eat a Turkey sandwich, and have a chocolate Malta for dessert.


Who is married to Antarctica?
*Uncle Arctica.*


Knock, knock.
*Who's there?*
India.
*India who?*
India nighttime I go to sleep.

Knock, knock.

*Who's there?*

Venice.

*Venice who?*

Venice this door going to open?


Why do paper maps never win poker
tournaments?

*Because they always fold.*


Where do pianists go for vacation?

*The Florida Keys.*


Knock, knock.

*Who's there?*

Jamaica.

*Jamaica who?*

Jamaica good grade on your geography test?

Why does Mississippi have the best vision out of all the states?

*Because it has four i's (eyes).*

**CAILEIGH:** Did Delaware a New Jersey?

**SHANNON:** I don't know, but Alaska.

Knock, knock.

*Who's there?*

Spain.

*Spain who?*

Spain to have to keep knocking on this door!


Where do Italian elephants live?

*Tusk-any.*

**TONGUE TWISTERS**

Miss Moss asks Missy to make a map
of Mississippi.

Kansas City's candy shops.

Intrepid tigers trekked to Texas.

Stella studied states studiously.

Hawaii hello: "Aloha!"

# Teacher Tee-Hee-Hees

Why did the teacher wear sunglasses in school?
*Because his class was so bright.*

What kind of cheese do teachers put on their pizza?

*Graded cheese.*

What do you call a teacher who never says your name right?

*Miss Pronounce.*

**WILL:** Would you be mad at me for something I didn't do?

**TEACHER:** Of course not.

**WILL:** That's good, because I forgot to do my homework!

What did the sweet potato say to the teacher?

*"Here I yam!"*

**TEACHER:** You should have been here at eight o'clock!

**MACY:** Why? What happened?

**TEACHER:** Carlie, please put more water in the fish tank.

**CARLIE:** But I put some in yesterday and he hasn't drunk that yet!

What did the cat teacher say to the cat student?

*"You have a purrrrfect score!"*

**SKYLAR:** How many pupils do you have?

**TEACHER:** Two, of course!

Knock, knock.

*Who's there?*

Ooze.

*Ooze who?*

Ooze in charge here?

**TEACHER:** Where's your homework, Zach?

**ZACH:** I don't have it. My dog ate it.

**TEACHER:** How could your dog eat your homework?

**ZACH:** I fed it to him.

What did the lobster give to its teacher?
*A crab apple.*

**CLEO:** I can see into the future.

**TEACHER:** How?

**CLEO:** I don't know. We'll find out tomorrow.


What happened when the teacher tied all the kids' shoelaces together?

*They had a class trip.*


**TEACHER:** Kim, I hope I didn't see you looking at Tory's exam.

**KIM:** I hope you didn't either.


What's the difference between a teacher and a train?

*A teacher says, "Spit out your gum." A train says, "Choo-choo!"*

**TEACHER:** Class, please turn in your cheese projects.

**KAELIN:** Why?

**TEACHER:** Because they will be grated.


Why did the teacher fall in love with the janitor?

*Because he swept her off her feet.*


**TEACHER:** What are you doing?

**JESSE:** I'm washing my hands.

**TEACHER:** Without soap and water?

**JESSE:** Haven't you heard of dry cleaning?


Why did the teacher write the lesson on the window?

*She wanted it to be perfectly clear.*

A student crawled into a classroom and the teacher asked, "Why are you crawling?"

He replied, "Because you told us not to dare walk into class late."

Why did the teacher go to the beach?
*To test the water.*

**TEACHER:** Name five things that contain milk.

**SANDRA:** Five cows.

**SCIENCE TEACHER:** Class, did you know that grasshoppers have antennas?

**MARIANNE:** Cool, do they get cable?

What's a teacher's favorite nation?
*Explanation.*

**MOM:** Why do you want to be a doctor, Sally?

**SALLY:** I wanted to be a teacher, but I don't have enough patience. I decided that I would be a doctor because then I can have all the patients I want.

**TEACHER:** We will have a half-day of school this morning.

**STUDENTS:** Hurray! Yippee!

**TEACHER:** We will have the other half this afternoon.

Knock, knock.

*Who's there?*

Razor.

*Razor who?*

Razor hand if you know the answer.

**TEACHER:** Keagan, why do you have cottonballs in your ears?

**KEAGAN:** You told me that everything you say goes in one ear and out the other. I'm just trying to keep it all in!

What did the teacher do with the cheese's homework?

*He grated it.*

**TEACHER:** What is the shortest month?

**GORDON:** May—it only has three letters.

What do teachers drink on snowy days?
*Hot chalk-olate.*

**PRINCIPAL:** Jordan, what have you been doing in class lately?

**JORDAN:** Nothing!

**PRINCIPAL:** That's exactly what your teacher said.

A teacher asked his class to give examples of coincidence. There was a long pause. Then a small boy said, "My father and mother were married on the same day."

What did the ghost teacher say to the class?
*"Look at the board and I will go through it again."*

When does a teacher carry birdseed?
*When she has a parrot-teacher conference.*

**TEACHER:** Ashley, you copied Kevin's answers on the test!

**ASHLEY:** How did you know?

**TEACHER:** Because on number 11, Kevin wrote, "I don't know," and you wrote, "Me neither."

What did the cheese teacher say to the cheese students at the end of the day?

*"You're dis-Swissed."*

**ANN:** Hooray! The teacher said we will have a test, rain or shine.

**DAN:** Then why are you so happy?

**ANN:** It's snowing!

**TEACHER:** Can you name something that didn't exist a hundred years ago?

**MARTIN:** Me!

What do you do if a teacher rolls her eyes at you?

*Pick them up and roll them back to her.*

**TEACHER:** Tanya, can you tell us the name of the mythical creature that is half-human, half-beast?

**TANYA:** Buffalo Bill!

What kind of dance do teachers like best?
*Attendance.*

**TEACHER:** What ever happened to that little chicken who kept misbehaving at school?

**PRINCIPAL:** She was eggspelled.

A teacher asked her students to draw cows eating grass. One student drew a cow on the paper with no grass. The teacher asked, "Why didn't you draw any grass?"

The student replied, "The cow ate it all!"

**TEACHER:** Everyone, pretend that you are a millionaire and write about how you feel.

*Tommy sits quietly, doing nothing.*

**TEACHER:** Tommy, why aren't you writing?

**TOMMY:** I'm waiting for my assistant to help me.

Why did the teacher write on the window?

*He wanted the lesson to be very clear.*

Knock, knock.

*Who's there?*

Raisin.

*Raisin who?*

We're raisin our hands before we speak.